Riddles and Brain Teasers for Clever Kids

Over 500 riddles for kids and their families

By Joshua Shifrin, PhD

Printed in the United States of America

First Printing, 2020

ISBN: 9781709427503

Dr. Joshua Shifrin

Shifrinbooks.com

-Dedication-

For Maya, Gilad, and Idan. You are my everything.

Table of Contents

Answers are on the back of each page!

-Introduction-

As a boy, some of my favorite childhood memories were sitting around the kitchen with my brother while we attempted to solve our parents' witty riddles. I loved the mental challenge of trying to solve these intellectual puzzles. In a small way, I actually believe that these brain exploring exercises led me to pursue my current career as a pediatric/school neuropsychologist where a large part of my job is to uncover the mysteries of the mind.

Now, as an adult, there is nothing I love more than spending time with my wife and two sons, while entertaining them with many of the riddles I attempted to solve myself years earlier. And even as my boys get older and pursue their independence, they are always willing to spend a few minutes with their old, fogy parents while attempting to answer a brain teaser or two.

I hope that you will find as much enjoyment from these riddles as they have brought to my family and me.

Easy Riddle Questions

1. What kind of coat can be put on only when wet?

2. What object has keys that open no locks, space but no room, and you can enter but can't go in?

3. What can be swallowed, but can also swallow you?

4. What two things can you never eat for breakfast?

5. They come out at night without being called, and are lost in the day without being stolen. What are they?

6. What can be put on a table and cut, but never eaten?

7. Inside a burning house, this thing is best to make. And best to make it quickly, before the fire is too much to take! What is it?

8. Susan has three daughters, and each of her daughters has a brother—how many children does Susan have?

Easy Riddle Answers

1. A coat of paint.

2. A computer keyboard.

3. Pride.

4. Lunch and dinner.

5. Stars.

6. A deck of cards.

7. Haste!

8. Four; each daughter has the same brother.

Easy Riddle Questions

9. When they are caught, they are thrown away. When they escape, you itch all day. What are they?

10. What kinds of stones are never found in the ocean?

11. Who is it that rows quickly with four oars but never comes out from under his own roof?

12. What is the worst vegetable to have on a ship?

13. What travels around the world but stays in one spot?

14. You have three stoves: a gas stove, a wood stove, and a coal stove but only one match. Which should you light first?

15. Which one of Santa's reindeer can be seen on Valentine's Day?

16. Mr. Blue lives in the blue house, Mr. Yellow lives in the yellow house, and Mr. Black lives in the black house. Who lives in the white house?

Easy Riddle Answers

9. Fleas.

10. Stones that are dry.

11. A turtle.

12. A leek (leak).

13. A stamp.

14. The match!

15. Cupid.

16. The President.

Easy Riddle Questions

17. A monkey, a squirrel, and a bird are racing to the top of a coconut tree. Who will get the banana first, the monkey, the squirrel, or the bird?

18. Why is an island similar to the letter T?

19. How can a pants pocket be completely empty and still have something in it?

20. What goes through towns and over hills but never moves?

21. What is something you will never see again?

22. Jack rode into town on Friday and rode out two days later on Friday. How can that be possible?

23. What is in the center of gravity?

24. A man was driving his car. His lights were not on. The moon was not out. In front of him a woman was crossing the street. How did he see her?

Easy Riddle Answers

17. None of them, because you cannot get a banana from a coconut tree!

18. Because they are both in the middle of water.

19. It can have a hole in it.

20. A road.

21. Yesterday.

22. Friday is his horse's name.

23. The letter V.

24. It was a bright and sunny day.

Easy Riddle Questions

25. How many months of the year have 28 days?

26. What five-letter word becomes shorter when you add two letters onto it?

27. How far can a bear run into the woods?

28. If a red house is made of red bricks, and a yellow house is made of yellow bricks, what is a greenhouse made of?

29. If two's company, and three's a crowd, what are four and five?

30. What goes up but never comes back down?

31. What begins with T, finishes with T, and has T in it?

32. Two girls have the same parents and were born at the same hour of the same day of the same month, but they are not twins. How can this be possible?

Easy Riddle Answers

25. All of them.

26. The word "short."

27. Only halfway, otherwise it would be running out of the woods!

28. Glass—all greenhouses are made of glass.

29. Nine.

30. Your age.

31. A teapot.

32. They were not born in the same year.

Easy Riddle Questions

33. What demands an answer but asks no question?

34. What falls but doesn't break, and what breaks but doesn't fall?

35. Why is swearing like an old coat?

36. What fastens two people yet touches only one?

37. Who are the two brothers who live on opposite sides of the road yet never see each other?

38. It's been around for millions of years, but it's no more than a month old. What is it?

39. Many things can create one, it can be of any shape or size, it is created for various reasons, and it can shrink or grow with time. What is it?

40. There is an ancient invention still used in some parts of the world today that allows people to see through walls. What is it?

Easy Riddle Answers

33. A telephone.

34. Night and day.

35. Because it is a bad habit.

36. A wedding ring.

37. Eyes.

38. The moon.

39. A hole.

40. A window.

Easy Riddle Questions

41. A doctor and a bus driver are both in love with the same woman, an attractive girl named Sarah. The bus driver had to go on a long bus trip that would last a week. Before he left, he gave Sarah seven apples. Why?

42. Why is Europe like a frying pan?

43. What do you call two witches who live together?

44. What did Mrs. Claus say to Santa when she looked up in the sky?

45. What did the baseball glove say to the ball?

46. When is a doctor most annoyed?

47. Which part of a road do ghosts love to travel the most?

48. What weighs more? A pound of feathers or a pound of stones?

Easy Riddle Answers

41. An apple a day keeps the doctor away!

42. Because it has Greece at the bottom.

43. Broommates!

44. Looks like rain dear.

45. Catch you later.

46. When he is out of patients.

47. The dead end.

48. The same. They both weigh a pound!

Easy Riddle Questions

49. What word is spelled wrong in every dictionary?

50. How can a leopard change its spots?

51. What answer can you never answer yes to?

52. I am the beginning of sorrow and the end of sickness. You cannot express happiness without me, yet I am in the midst of crosses. I am always in risk, yet never in danger. You may find me in the sun, but I am never out of darkness.

53. How many letters are there in the English alphabet?

54. Johnny throws a ball as hard as he can. It comes back to him, even though it touches nothing. How?

55. If a fender cost $6 dollars, what will a ton of coal come to?

56. What stays where it is when it goes off?

Easy Riddle Answers

49. Wrong.

50. By moving from one spot to another spot.

51. Are you sleeping?

52. The letter S.

53. 18: 3 in "the," 7 in "English," and 8 in "alphabet."

54. He throws it straight up.

55. To ashes.

56. A cannon.

Easy Riddle Questions

57. Before Mount Everest was discovered, what was the highest mountain on Earth?

58. What runs around the whole yard without moving?

59. I never was; I am always to be. No one ever saw me nor ever will, and yet I am the confidence of all to live and breathe on this terrestrial ball.

60. What kind of running means walking?

61. How do you make "one" disappear?

62. Which bird does not belong in this group? Finch, gull, eagle, ostrich, or sparrow?

63. What did the tree wear to the pool?

64. What four-letter word can be written forward, backward, or upside down, and can still be read from left to right?

Easy Riddle Answers

57. Mount Everest.

58. A fence.

59. I am tomorrow—your future.

60. Running out of gas!

61. Add a G and you're gone!

62. The ostrich. It's the only bird that doesn't fly.

63. Swim trunks!

64. NOON. Cool, huh?

Easy Riddle Questions

65. After drawing a line, how do you make it a longer line without touching it?

66. What begins and ends with the letter E but only has one letter in it?

67. What is easy to get into but hard to get out of?

68. If a man wasn't under an umbrella, why didn't he get wet?

69. Michael's parents have three sons: Snap, Crackle and...?

70. What word starting with the letters BR, that with the addition of the letter E, becomes another word that sounds the same as the first?

71. If you are running in a race and you pass the person in second place, what place are you in?

72. Why did my father remind me to bring two pairs of pants when we go golfing this weekend?

Easy Riddle Answers

65. Draw a shorter line next to it, and now it will become the longer line.

66. An envelope.

67. Trouble.

68. It wasn't raining.

69. Michael.

70. Braking becomes breaking.

71. Second place.

72. In case I get a hole in 1.

Easy Riddle Questions

73. What gets wetter the more it dries?

74. What's the difference between a jeweler and a jailer?

75. Walk on the living, they don't even mumble. Walk on the dead, they mutter and grumble. What are they?

76. What word contains all of the 26 letters?

77. What has a head but never weeps, has a bed but never sleeps, can run but never walks, and has a bank but no money?

78. A man leaves home and turns left three times, only to return home facing two men wearing masks. Who are those two men?

79. You give someone a dollar. You are this person's brother, but the person is not your brother. How can that be?

80. Where on Earth do the winds always blow from the South?

Easy Riddle Answers

73. A towel.

74. A jeweler sells watches, and a jailer watches cells.

75. Fallen leaves.

76. Alphabet.

77. A river.

78. A catcher and an umpire.

79. It's your sister!

80. The North Pole.

Easy Riddle Questions

81. Mary's father has five daughters: Nana, Nene, Nini, and Nono. What is the fifth daughter's name?

82. What kind of tree can you carry in your hand?

83. If an electric train is travelling south, which way is the smoke going?

84. What is the last thing you take off before going to bed?

85. If you threw a white stone into the Red Sea, what would it become?

86. What invention lets you look right through a wall?

87. What has four legs but can't walk?

88. Three men were in a boat. It capsized, but only two got their hair wet. Why?

Easy Riddle Answers

81. If you answered Nunu, you are wrong. It is Mary!

82. A palm.

83. There is no smoke; it is an electric train!

84. Your feet off the floor.

85. Wet.

86. A window.

87. A table.

88. One was bald.

Easy Riddle Questions

89. What common English verb becomes its own past tense by rearranging its letters?

90. How can you physically stand behind your friend as he physically stands behind you?

91. What do you use to hoe a row, slay a foe, and wring with woe?

92. Where will you find roads without cars, forests without trees, and cities without houses?

93. Why are 1990 dollar bills worth more than 1989 dollar bills?

94. Where do turkeys go to dance?

95. If a fire hydrant has H2O inside, what does it have on the outside?

96. If you drop a yellow hat in the Red Sea, what does it become?

Easy Riddle Answers

89. Eat and ate.

90. By standing back to back.

91. Your hands.

92. On a map.

93. The same reason seven dollars is more than six. Because there is one more.

94. The Butter Ball.

95. K9P (you'll get it eventually).

96. Wet, duh!

Easy Riddle Questions

97. What is so delicate that saying its name breaks it?

98. After a plane crashed, every single person died. Who survived?

99. A word I know, six letters it contains, remove one letter, and twelve remains. What is it?

100. When things go wrong, what can you always count on?

101. What is always ahead of you but can't be seen?

102. Where can you find streets, towns, and cities but no people?

103. What has a neck but no head?

104. Why would a man living in New York not be buried in Chicago?

Easy Riddle Answers

97.   Silence.

98.   The couples.

99.   Dozens.

100.   Your fingers.

101.   The future.

102.   A map.

103.   A bottle.

104.   Because he is still living.

Easy Riddle Questions

105. You live in a one-story house made entirely of redwood. What color would the stairs be?

106. What is more useful when it is broken?

107. Where does success come before work?

108. What is black when you buy it, red when you use it, and gray when you throw it away?

109. What can be heard and caught but never seen?

110. It speaks with a hard tongue; it cannot breathe, for it has no lung. What is it?

111. If a rooster laid a brown egg and a white egg, what kind of chicks would hatch?

112. What can go up and come down without moving?

Easy Riddle Answers

105. What stairs? You live in a one-story house.

106. An egg.

107. Only in the dictionary.

108. Charcoal.

109. A remark.

110. A bell.

111. Roosters don't lay eggs.

112. The temperature.

Easy Riddle Questions

113. What five-letter word typed in all capital letters can be read the same upside down?

114. What do you call cheese that belongs to someone else?

115. Why was the picture sent to jail?

116. What room do ghosts avoid?

117. Why was the broom late?

118. What word doesn't belong in this group? That, hat, what, mat, cat, sat, pat, or chat?

119. What gets whiter the dirtier it gets?

120. What is the difference between a school boy studying and a farmer watching his cattle?

Easy Riddle Answers

113. SWIMS.

114. Nacho cheese!

115. Because it was framed.

116. The living room.

117. It overswept.

118. What. It's pronounced differently; all the others rhyme.

119. A chalkboard.

120. One is stocking his mind, while the other is minding his stock.

Easy Riddle Questions

121. What has many keys, but can't even open a single door?

122. When will water stop running down hill?

123. A hundred feet in the air, but it's back is on the ground. What is it?

124. What never gets any wetter, no matter how much it rains?

125. What always goes to bed with shoes on?

126. I am white, black, and read all over. What am I?

127. What animal keeps the best time?

128. No matter how little or how much you use me, you change me every month. What am I?

Easy Riddle Answers

121. A piano.

122. When it reaches the bottom.

123. A centipede flipped over.

124. The sea.

125. A horse.

126. Newspaper!

127. A watchdog.

128. A calendar.

Easy Riddle Questions

129. What ship has two mates but no captain?

130. What kind of room has no doors or windows?

131. What goes up when the rain comes down?

132. When is it bad luck to see a black cat?

133. What does a snowman like to eat for breakfast?

134. What time does a tennis player get up?

135. How can you leave a room with two legs and return with six legs?

136. Why should a fisherman be very wealthy?

Easy Riddle Answers

129. A relationship.

130. A mushroom.

131. An umbrella.

132. When you are a mouse.

133. Frosted Flakes.

134. Ten-ish.

135. Bring a chair back with you.

136. Because he has all net profit.

Easy Riddle Questions

137. What do you serve that you can't eat?

138. What can be seen in the middle of March and April that cannot be seen at the beginning or end of either month?

139. What never asks questions but is often answered?

140. What belongs to you, but other people use it more than you?

141. What four-letter word becomes longer when you add two letters to it?

142. When does Christmas come before Thanksgiving?

143. What can point in every direction but can't reach the destination by itself.

144. What has no beginning, end, or middle?

Easy Riddle Answers

137. A tennis ball.

138. The letter R.

139. A doorbell.

140. Your name.

141. Long.

142. In the dictionary.

143. Your finger.

144. A doughnut.

Easy Riddle Questions

145. What is it that is deaf, dumb, and blind, and always tells the truth?

146. What did the bee say to the flower?

147. What's a lifeguard's favorite game?

148. What can you catch but not throw?

149. Why did the mother put wheels on her rocking chair?

150. What says who but never why and when?

Easy Riddle Answers

145. A mirror.

146. Hello, honey!

147. Pool.

148. A cold.

149. She still likes to rock and roll.

150. An owl.

"What Am I?" Riddles

151. I go up, and I go down. I am blazing and hot. If you look right at me, your eyes will wish you had not. What am I?

152. I can be white or dark, and sweet or bitter, and you often find me on a dessert. What am I?

153. You can slice and dice me, chop and peel me. I can be cut or cooked, and I might make you cry. What am I?

154. I have hands, but I can't clap. What am I?

155. I have to be broken before you can use me. What am I?

156. I'm tall when I'm young, and I'm short when I'm old. What am I?

157. You bought me for lunch but will never eat me. What am I?

158. I have four eyes, but I am unable to see. What am I?

"What Am I?" Answers

151. The sun.

152. Chocolate.

153. An onion.

154. A clock.

155. An egg.

156. A candle.

157. Silverware.

158. Mississippi.

"What Am I?" Riddles

159. I move very slowly at an imperceptible rate. Although I take my time, I am never late. I accompany life and survive past demise; I am viewed with esteem in many women's eyes. What am I?

160. I am full of holes but still hold water. What am I?

161. I am always there for you, following you around on sunny days. I copy everything you do, and lot of times you see me on the ground. What am I?

162. I can be small or big on a ceiling, but I can shine and light up everyone's home at night. What am I?

163. I am shorter than all my pals, and every four years on the calendar I change just a bit and throw everyone off. What am I?

164. I can be long or short, thick or thin, full or sparse, and you can color it anything you want? What am I?

165. I am black and white and blue? What am I?

"What Am I?" Answers

159. I am your hair.

160. A sponge.

161. Your shadow.

162. A light bulb.

163. February.

164. Hair.

165. A sad zebra.

"What Am I?" Riddles

166. I speak without a mouth and hear without ears. I have no body, but I come alive with wind. What am I?

167. I have three feet, but I can't stand without leaning. To make matters worse I have no arms to lean with. Please be good so that I'm not called into use. What am I?

168. I'm not really more than holes tied to more holes; I'm strong as good steel, though not as stiff as a pole. What am I?

169. Pronounced as one letter and written with three; two letters there are, and two only in me. I'm double, I'm single, I can be brown, blue or green. I'm read from both ends, and the same either way. What am I?

170. I can be served but never eaten. What am I?

171. I go up and down but never move. What am I?

172. I start with the letter P and end with the letter E and have thousands of letters. What am I?

"What Am I?" Answers

166. An echo.

167. A yardstick.

168. A chain.

169. An eye.

170. A tennis ball.

171. The temperature or a flight of stairs.

172. The post office.

"What Am I?" Riddles

173. I am not alive, but I grow; I don't have lungs, but I need air; I don't have a mouth, but water kills me. What am I?

174. I smell bad when I'm living but good when I'm dead. What am I?

175. I am taken from a mine and shut up in a wooden case from which I am never released, and yet I am used by almost everybody. What am I?

176. The one who made it didn't want it. The one who bought it didn't need it. The one who used it never saw it. What is it?

177. I can make two people out of one person. What am I?

178. I have a neck but no head, two arms but no hands, and you see me every day. What am I?

179. I live on a farm. I run all around the farm, but I never move. What am I?

"What Am I?" Answers

173. Fire.

174. Bacon.

175. Pencil lead.

176. A coffin.

177. A mirror.

178. A shirt.

179. A fence.

"What Am I?" Riddles

180. I don't live, but I can die. What am I?

181. What kind of man can shave 10 times a day but still has a beard?

182. I am an instrument you can hear but never see? What am I?

183. My life can be measured in hours; I serve by being devoured. Thin, I am quick. Fat, I am slow. Wind is my foe. What am I?

184. I have cities, but no houses. I have mountains, but no trees. I have water, but no fish. What am I?

185. They have not flesh, nor feathers, nor scales, nor bone. Yet they have fingers and thumbs of their own. What are they?

186. I am large as a castle, yet lighter than air. One hundred men and their horses cannot move me. What am I?

"What Am I?" Answers

180. A battery.

181. A barber.

182. Your voice!

183. I am a candle.

184. A map.

185. Gloves.

186. The castle's shadow.

"What Am I?" Riddles

187. I have two hands, but I cannot scratch myself. What am I?

188. I can be cracked, I can be made. I can be told, I can be played. What am I?

189. I have no feet, no hands, and no wings, but I climb to the sky. What am I?

190. If you have me, you want to share me. If you share me, you haven't got me. What am I?

191. If I surround you, I can kill you. What am I?

192. I'm as small as an ant, as big as a whale. I'll approach like a breeze but can come like a gale. By some I get hit, but all have shown fear. I'll dance to the music, though I can't hear. Of names I have many, of names I have one. I'm as slow as a snail, but from me you can't run. What am I?

193. I will burn the eyes, sting the mouth, yet be consumed? What am I?

"What Am I?" Answers

187. A clock.

188. A joke!

189. Smoke.

190. A secret.

191. Water.

192. I am a shadow.

193. Salt.

"What Am I?" Riddles

194. I am an odd number. Take away a letter and I become even. What number am I?

195. My voice is tender, my waist is slender, and I'm often invited to play. Yet wherever I go, I must take my bow, or else I have nothing to say. What am I?

196. I start with an A and end with an A. I have many states inside of me. What am I?

197. You use a knife to slice my head and weep beside me when I am dead. What am I?

198. This is as light as a feather, yet no man can hold it for long. What am I?

199. I pass before the sun, yet make no shadow. What am I?

200. What can run but never walks, has a mouth but never talks, has a head but never weeps, has a bed but never sleeps?

"What Am I?" Answers

194. Seven.

195. A violin.

196. America.

197. An onion.

198. Your breath.

199. The wind.

200. A river.

"What Am I?" Riddles

201. I killed one fourth of all mankind. Who am I?

202. I have a heart that never beats; I have a home, but I never sleep. I can take a man's house and build another's, and I love to play games with my many brothers. I am a king among fools. Who am I?

203. With pointed fangs it sits in wait, with piercing force its doles out fate, over bloodless victims proclaiming its might, eternally joining in a single bite. What am I?

204. When I point up, it is bright, but when I point down, it is dark. What am I?

205. I am white when I am dirty and black when I am clean. What am I?

206. I can be a king or queen, single or double and remain covered most of the day. What am I?

"What Am I?" Answers

201. Cain (who killed Abel).

202. The king of hearts in a deck of cards.

203. A stapler.

204. A light switch.

205. A blackboard.

206. A bed.

"What Am I?" Riddles

207. I have wings, and I have a tail, across the sky is where I sail. Yet I have no eyes, ears, or mouth, and I bob randomly from north to south. What am I?

208. I come in many different colors, and I get bigger when I'm full. I will float away if you don't tie me down, and I will make a loud sound if I break. What am I?

209. I have a thumb and four fingers, but I am not alive? What am I?

210. I am round or oval. I can be light or dark. You can cut me in pieces. What am I?

211. I have one eye but can't see. What am I?

212. Forward I am heavy, but backward I am not. What am I?

213. The more you take, the more you leave behind. What are they?

"What Am I?" Answers

207. A kite

208. A balloon.

209. A glove.

210. A potato.

211. A needle

212. Ton

213. Footprints.

"What Am I?" Riddles

214. You bought me for dinner but never eat me. What am I?

215. A very pretty thing am I, fluttering in the pale-blue sky. Delicate, fragile on the wing, indeed I am a pretty thing. What am I?

216. I was carried into a dark room and set on fire. I wept, and then my head was cut off. What am I?

217. Mountains will crumble and temples will fall, and no man can survive its endless call. What is it?

218. This old one runs forever but never moves at all. It has not lungs nor throat, but still a mighty roaring call. What is it?

219. What can go up a chimney down, but cannot go down a chimney up?

220. The more there is the less you see. What is it?

"What Am I?" Answers

214. Cutlery.

215. I am a butterfly.

216. A candle.

217. Time.

218. A waterfall.

219. An umbrella.

220. Fog.

"What Am I?" Riddles

221. You can carry it everywhere you go, and it does not get heavy. What is it?

222. I have a little house in which I live all alone. It has no doors or windows, and if I want to go out, I must break through the wall. What am I?

223. I'm white, and used for cutting and grinding. When I'm damaged, humans usually remove me or fill me. For most animals I am a useful tool. What am I?

224. A time when they are green, a time when they're brown, but both of these times cause me to frown. But just in between, for a very short while, they're perfect and yellow and cause me to smile! What am I?

225. The more you take away, the more I become. What am I?

226. It stands on one leg with its heart in its head. What is it?

"What Am I?" Answers

221. Your name.

222. A chick in an egg.

223. A tooth!

224. Bananas.

225. A hole.

226. A cabbage.

"What Am I?" Riddles

227. There was a green house. Inside the green house there was a white house. Inside the white house there was a red house. Inside the red house there are lots of babies. What am I?

228. Poke your fingers in my eyes, and I will open wide my jaws. Linen cloth, quills, or paper, my greedy lust devours them all. What am I?

229. A cloud was my mother, the wind is my father. My son is the cool stream, and my daughter is the fruit of the land. A rainbow is my bed, the earth is my final resting place, and I'm the torment of man. Who am I?

230. I am one with eight to spare, lest I lose my one. I'm not a number. What am I?

231. I am inanimate, yet I can stand up. I can start out copper and end up as steel. I'm so fragile, a child could break me. But many of me have the strength to lift a man? What am I?

"What Am I?" Answers

227. A watermelon.

228. Shears, or scissors.

229. Rain.

230. A cat (nine lives).

231. A human hair.

"What Am I?" Riddles

232. You pick me, peel the outside, cook the inside, eat the outside, and throw away the inside. What am I?

233. I'm a word that's hardly there. Take away my start, and I'm an herbal flair. What am I?

234. I have holes on the top and bottom. I have holes on my left and on my right. And I have holes in the middle, yet I still hold water. What am I?

235. Who spends the day at the window, goes to the table for meals, and hides at night?

236. What is that goes with a car, comes with a car, is of no use to a car, and yet the car cannot go without it. What is it?

237. Dark with white markings and smooth like a rock. Where learning occurs, I help convey thought. What am I?

"What Am I?" Answers

232. Corn.

233. Sparsely (no S = parsley).

234. A sponge.

235. A fly.

236. Noise.

237. Blackboard/chalkboard.

"What Am I?" Riddles

238. I have four wings but cannot fly. I never laugh and never cry. On the same spot I'm always found, toiling away with little sound. What am I?

239. I have many feathers to help me fly. I have a body and a head, but I'm not alive. It is your strength that determines how far that I go. You can hold me in your hand, but I'm never thrown. What am I?

240. You must keep this thing; its loss will affect your brothers. For once yours is lost, it will soon be lost by others. What is it?

241. I have a little pool with two layers of wall around me. One is white and soft; the other dark and hard amid a light brown, grassy lawn with an outline of green grass. What am I?

242. Take one out and scratch my head. I am now black but once was red. What am I?

"What Am I?" Answers

238. A windmill.

239. An arrow.

240. Your temper.

241. A coconut.

242. A match.

"What Am I?" Riddles

243. Violet, indigo, blue, and green; yellow, orange, and red. These are the colors you have seen after the storm has fled. What am I?

244. In spring I am gay in handsome array; in summer more clothing I wear; when colder it grows I fling off my clothes; and in winter I appear quite naked. What am I?

245. Old Mother Twitchett had but one eye and a long tail which she let fly. Every time she went through a gap, a bit of her tail she left in a trap. What is she?

246. Never resting, never still. Moving silently from hill to hill. It does not walk, run or trot; all is cool where it is not. What is it?

247. He has married many women, but has never been married. Who is he?

"What Am I?" Answers

243. I am a rainbow.

244. A tree.

245. A needle and thread.

246. Sunshine.

247. A preacher.

"What Am I?" Riddles

248. It goes up but at the same time goes down. Up toward the sky and down toward the ground. It's present tense and past tense, too; come for a ride, just me and you. What is it?

249. I cover what's real, hide what is true, but sometimes bring out the courage in you. What am I?

250. I build up castles. I tear down mountains. I make some men blind. I help others to see. What am I?

251. Lovely and round, I shine with pale light, grown in the darkness, a lady's delight. What am I?

252. At the sound of me, men may dream or stamp their feet. At the sound of me, women may laugh or sometimes weep. What am I?

253. You can see nothing else when you look in my face. I will look you in the eye, and I will never lie. What am I?

"What Am I?" Answers

248. A see-saw.

249. Makeup.

250. I am sand.

251. A pearl.

252. I am music!

253. I am your reflection.

"What Am I?" Riddles

254. Three lives have I. Gentle enough to soothe the skin, light enough to caress the sky, and hard enough to crack rocks. What am I?

255. You heard me before, yet you hear me again, then I die until you call me again. What am I?

256. From the beginning of eternity to the end of time and space, to the beginning of every end and the end of every place. What am I?

257. When you stop and look, you can always see me. If you try to touch, you cannot feel me. I cannot move, but as you near me, I will move away from you. What am I?

258. Look at me. I can bring a smile to your face, a tear to your eye, or even a thought to your mind. But I can't be seen. What am I?

"What Am I?" Answers

254. I am water.

255. I am an echo.

256. The letter E.

257. I am the horizon.

258. Your memories.

"What Am I?" Riddles

259. I am served at a table, small, white and round, in gatherings of two or four. You'll love some, and that's part of the fun. What am I?

260. I turn around once. What is out will not get in. I turn around again. What is in will not get out. What am I?

261. I never was, am always to be. No one ever saw me, nor ever will, and yet I am the confidence of all to live and breathe on this terrestrial ball. What am I?

262. Some will use me, while others will not; some have remembered, while others have forgotten. For profit or gain, I'm used expertly; I can't be picked off the ground or tossed into the sea. Only gained from patience and time, can you unravel my rhyme? What am I?

"What Am I?" Answers

259. Ping-Pong balls.

260. A key.

261. Tomorrow.

262. I'm knowledge.

"What Am I?" Riddles

263. Hands she has but does not hold, teeth she has but does not bite, feet she has but they are cold, eyes she has but without sight. Who is she?

264. I make you weak at the worst of all times. I keep you safe, I keep you fine. I make your hands sweat, and your heart grow cold. I visit the weak but seldom the bold. What am I?

265. This thing runs but cannot walk, sometimes sings but never talks. Lacks arms, but has hands; lacks a head but has a face. What is it?

266. I have no voice and yet I speak to you. I tell of all things in the world that people do. I have leaves, but I am not a tree. I have pages, but I am not a bride or royalty. I have a spine and hinges, but I am not a man or a door. I have told you all, I cannot tell you more. What am I?

267. You use it between your head and toes. The more it works, the thinner it grows. What is it?

"What Am I?" Answers

263. A doll.

264. Your fears.

265. A clock.

266. A book.

267. A bar of soap.

"What Am I?" Riddles

268. They have not flesh, feathers, scales, or bone. Yet they have fingers and thumbs of their own. What are they?

269. If a man carried my burden, he would break his back. I am not big but leave silver in my tracks. What am I?

270. Until I am measured, I am not known. Yet how you miss me when I have flown. What am I?

271. I dig out tiny caves and store gold and silver in them. I also build bridges of silver and make crowns of gold. They are the smallest you could imagine. Sooner or later everybody needs my help, yet many people are afraid to let me help them. Who am I?

272. Be you ever so quick with vision keen; by your eyes, we are never seen. Unless perchance it should come to pass, you see our reflection in a looking glass. What are we?

"What Am I?" Answers

268. Gloves.

269. A snail.

270. Time.

271. I am a dentist.

272. Your own eyes.

Math Riddles

273. When you add eight 8s, the result you get will be the number 1,000. How is it possible? You are permitted to use only addition to solve the problem.

274. Two hens can lay two eggs in 2 minutes. If this is the maximum speed possible, what is the total number of hens needed to get 500 eggs in 500 minutes?

275. When Ravi was asked how old he was, he replied: "In a period of two years, my age will be twice my age when you asked this five years ago." How old is he?

276. If there are three apples, and you take away two, how many do you have?

277. What do the numbers 11, 69, and 88 all have in common?

278. If you multiply me by any other number, the answer will always remain the same. What number am I?

279. If four people can repair four bicycles in four hours, how many bicycles can eight people repair in eight hours?

Math Riddles Answers

273. 888 + 88 + 8 + 8 + 8 = 1,000

274. Two hens.

275. 12.

276. If you take two apples, then, of course, you have two.

277. They read the same right side up and upside down.

278. Zero.

279. 16 bicycles.

Math Riddles

280. How can you make seven even?

281. Three plus four is seven. But five plus eight is one. How is this possible?

282. Mr. and Mrs. Mustard have six daughters, and each daughter has one brother. How many people are in the Mustard family?

283. When can you add two to eleven and get one as the correct answer?

284. Give me an X, I'll stand to face you. Give me a cross, I'll turn my back on you. What am I?

285. Farmer Brown came to town with some watermelons. He sold half of them, plus half a melon, and found that he had one whole melon left. How many melons did he take to town?

286. A large truck is crossing a bridge 1 mile long. The bridge can only hold 14,000 pounds, which is the exact weight of the truck. The truck makes it halfway across the bridge and stops. A bird lands on the truck. Does the bridge collapse?

Math Riddles Answers

280. Remove the letter S.

281. You are looking at a clock.

282. There are nine Mustards in the family. Since each daughter shares the same brother, there are six girls, one boy, and Mr. and Mrs. Mustard.

283. When you add two hours to 11 o'clock, you get 1 o'clock.

284. The number 9 (9 x 9 = 81 and 9 + 9 = 18).

285. Easy, three melons!

286. No, it does not collapse, because it has driven a half mile. You would subtract the gas used from the total weight of the truck.

Math Riddles

287. Two fathers and two sons sat down to eat eggs for breakfast. They ate exactly three eggs, and each person had an egg. Explain how?

288. Divide 110 into two parts so that one will be 150 percent of the other. What are the two numbers?

289. There are a mix of red, green, and blue balls in a bag. The total number of balls is 60. There are four times as many red balls as green balls, and six more blue balls than green balls. How many balls of each color are there?

290. How many times can you subtract the number 5 from 25?

291. The ages of a father and son add up to 66. The father's age is the son's age reversed. How old could they be?

292. I am a three-digit number. My tens digit is five more than my ones digit. My hundreds digit is eight less than my tens digit. What number am I?

293. Why is six afraid of seven?

Math Riddles Answers

287. One of the "fathers" is also a grandfather. Therefore, the other father is both a son and a father to the grandson. In other words, the one father is both a son and a father.

288. 44 and 66.

289. Blue balls = 15 red balls = 36 green balls = 9.

290. Only once. After the first calculation, you will be subtracting 5 from 20, then 5 from 15, and so on.

291. 51 and 15, 42 and 24, 60 and 06.

292. 194.

293. Because seven eight nine!

Math Riddles

294. Add the number to the number itself, and then multiply by four. Again divide the number by eight and you will get the same number once more. Which is that number?

295. At the time of shipping, Mark can place 10 small boxes or eight large boxes into a container. A total of 96 boxes were sent in one shipment. The number of small boxes was less than the large boxes. What is the total number of containers he shipped?

296. You are given three positive numbers. You can add these numbers or multiply them together, and you will get the same result. Which are the numbers?

297. I have a large barrel of wine, and your job is to measure out 1 gallon from it. I can give you a 5-gallon container and 3-gallon container. How can you get 1 gallon?

298. Mary was asked to paint the numbers on doors of 100 apartments, which means she will have to paint numbers 1 through 100. Can you figure out the number of times Mary will have to paint the number eight?

Math Riddles Answers

294. Any number.

295. 11 containers, 4 small boxes (4 x 10 = 40 boxes), 7 large boxes (7 x 8 = 56 boxes). So, he shipped 96 boxes and 11 total containers.

296. 1, 2 and 3.

297. First fill up the 3-gallon container with wine. Then transfer the 3 gallons to the 5-gallon container. Then fill up the 3-gallon container again, and transfer the wine to the 5-gallon container until it is full. The left-over in the 3-gallon container measures 1 gallon.

298. 20 times (8, 18, 28, 38, 48, 58, 68, 78, 80, 81, 82, 83, 84, 85, 86, 87, 88, 89, 98).

Math Riddles

299. I am a three-digit number. My second digit is four times bigger than the third digit. My first digit is three less than my second digit. What is the answer?

300. You are given a telephone and asked to multiply all the numbers on the number pad. What will be the answer?

301. I have a pound of feathers and a pound of bricks? Which one weighs more?

302. Maya tossed a coin 10 times, and it landed in the heads-up position all 10 times. What are the chances that if she tosses it one more time, it will land in the heads-up position?

303. There are six black socks, eight white socks, four brown socks, and two red socks in my sock drawer. Can you figure out the minimum number of socks I would have to pull out to get a matching pair?

304. How many times can you subtract the number 5 from 25?

Math Riddles Answers

299. 141.

300. Zero. (The number pad contains the number 0. When you multiply any number by zero, the answer will be zero.)

301. Both of them would be of same weight. A pound remains a pound despite the type of object.

302. She has a 50 percent chance to toss the coin and see the heads-up position. This is because the coin toss is not dependent on the first 10 tosses.

303. At least five.

304. Once, because after you subtract, it's not 25 anymore.

Math Riddles

305. A man is twice as old as his little sister. He is also half as old as their dad. Over a period of 50 years, the age of the sister will become half of their dad's age. What is the age of the man now?

306. Brian and Bobby live in different parts of city but go to the same high school. Brian left for school 10 minutes before Bobby started, and they happened to meet at a park. At the time of their meeting, who was closer to the school?

307. Seven girls met each other in a party. Each of them shakes hands only once with each of the other girls. What is the total number of handshakes that took place?

308. Margaret has two children. If the older child is a boy, then what is the possibility that her other child is also a boy?

309. When my dad was 31 years old, I was just 8 years. Now his age is twice as old as my age. What is my current age?

Math Riddles Answers

305. He is 50 years old.

306. They are both the same distance from school because they met in the same place.

307. 21.

308. 50 percent.

309. When you calculate the difference between the ages, you can see that it is 23 years. So you must be 23 years old now.

Math Riddles

310. If you go to the movies and you're paying, is it cheaper to take one friend to the movies twice, or two friends to the movies at the same time?

311. A tree doubled in height each year until it reached its maximum height over the course of 10 years. How many years did it take for the tree to reach half its maximum height?

312. When asked how old she was, Suzie replied, "In two years, I will be twice as old as I was five years ago." How old is she?

313. A man decides to buy a nice horse. He pays $600 for it, and he is very content with this strong animal. After a year, the value of the horse has increased to $700, and he decides to sell the horse. But already a few days later he regrets his decision to sell the beautiful horse, and he buys it again. Unfortunately he has to pay $800 to get it back, so he loses $100. After another year of owning the horse, he finally decides to sell the horse for $900. What is the overall profit the man makes?

314. My age today is three times what it will be three years from now minus three times what my age was three years ago. How old am I?

Math Riddles Answers

310. It's cheaper to take two friends at the same time. In this case, you would only be buying three tickets, whereas if you take the same friend twice, you are buying four tickets.

311. Nine years.

312. She's 12!

313. The man makes an overall profit of $200.

314. Don't be too confused; the answer is 18 years old.

Math Riddles

315. What has one foot on each side and one in the middle?

316. How many 3-cent stamps are in a dozen?

317. What is the value of 1/2 of 2/3 of 3/4 of 4/5 of 5/6 of 6/7 of 7/8 of 8/9 of 9/10 of 1,000?

318. There is a clothing store in Bartlesville. The owner has devised his own method of pricing items. A vest costs $20, socks cost $25, a tie costs $15, and a blouse costs $30. Using the same method, how much would a pair of underwear cost?

319. If three cats catch three mice in 3 minutes, how many cats would be needed to catch 100 mice in 100 minutes?

320. If someone says to you, "I'll bet you $1 that if you give me $2, I will give you $3 in return," would this be a good bet for you to accept?

Math Riddles Answers

315. A yardstick.

316. A dozen, although you probably said four.

317. One hundred: Work backwards and you will understand.

318. $45. The pricing method consists of charging $5 for each letter required to spell the item.

319. The same three cats would do. Since these three cats are averaging one mouse per minute, given 100 minutes, the cats could catch 100 mice.

320. No. This is a situation where you lose even if you win. Assuming the other person is being wise, they would take your $2 and say, "I lose," and give you $1 in return. You win the bet, but you're out $1.

Math Riddles

321. If you have three oranges, and you take away two, how many will you have?

322. What is the difference between a dollar and a half and 30 5-cents?

323. A car's odometer shows 72927 miles, a palindromic number. What is the minimum number of miles you would need to travel to form another?

324. A customer wants to buy himself a new car. He picks out a BMW for $27,000. The customer buys it without paying a dime. How is that possible?

325. Steven has a toaster with two spaces for bread so he can toast one side each of two breads at the same time, which takes 1 minute. If he wants to make three pieces of toast, what is the minimum time required to do so?

Math Riddles Answers

321. Two. The two you took.

322. Nothing. A dollar and a half is the same as 30 5-cents (nickels). But not the same as 35 cents.

323. 110 miles. (73037)

324. He didn't pay a dime; he paid $27,000.

325. Three minutes! First, Steven can put two pieces of bread in the toaster. After 1 minute, one side each of the two breads will get toasted. He can then flip a side of bread and take the other one out. Then he can place the third piece of bread into the free space of the toaster. After the second minute, he can take the completely toasted bread out and flip the other one. Then place the half-toasted bread into the free space to toast the fresh side. After 3 minutes, all three pieces of bread get toasted.

Mystery Riddles

326. There once was an evil wizard. He took three women from their homes and turned them into rose bushes that looked exactly alike. Then he put them in his garden. One of the women had a husband and children and begged the wizard to let her see them. He agreed. At night, he brought the woman to her house. In the morning he came and took her home. One day the husband decided to go rescue her. So he snuck into the wizard's garden. He looked and looked at the three identical rose bushes trying to figure out which could be his wife. Suddenly, he knew the answer, and he took his wife home. How did he know which rose bush was his wife?

327. A man was shot to death while in his car. There were no powder marks on his clothing, which indicated that the gunman was outside the car. However, all the windows were up and the doors locked. After a close inspection was made, the only bullet holes discovered were on the man's body. How was he murdered?

328. If I have it, I don't share it. If I share it, I don't have it. What is it?

Mystery Riddle Answers

326. The wizard brought the rose bush to her home at night and returned her to the garden in the morning. Therefore, she was the only plant without dew.

327. The victim was in a convertible. He was shot when the top was down.

328. A secret.

Mystery Riddles

329. An old man wanted to leave all his money to one of his three sons, but he didn't know which one he should give it to. He gave each of them a few coins and told them to buy something that would be able to fill their living room. The first man bought straw, but there was not enough to fill the room. The second bought some sticks, but they still did not fill the room. The third man bought two things that filled the room, so he obtained his father's fortune. What were the two things that the man bought?

330. You're in a magical bathroom with no windows, and the only way things can get in and out is by an open door. You decide to take a bath, so you turn on the tap. You shut the door, and the handle breaks, so you can't open it. You then turn off the tap, and the knob breaks so water keeps coming. How do you save yourself from drowning?

331. A man was found murdered on Sunday morning. His wife immediately called the police. The police questioned the wife and staff and got their alibis. The wife said she was sleeping. The cook was cooking breakfast. The gardener was picking vegetables. The maid was getting the mail. The butler was cleaning the closet. The police instantly arrested the murderer. Who did it, and how did they know?

Mystery Riddle Answers

329. The wise son bought a candle and a box of matches. After lighting the candle, the light filled the entire room.

330. Pull out the plug in the bath.

331. It was the maid. She said she was getting the mail. There is no mail on Sunday!

Mystery Riddles

332. A traveler, on his way to Miami, reaches a road junction, where he can turn left or right. He knows that only one of the two roads leads to Miami, but unfortunately, he does not know which one. Fortunately, he sees two twin brothers standing at the road junction, and he decides to ask them for directions. The traveler knows that one of the two brothers always tells the truth, and the other one always lies. Unfortunately, he does not know which one always tells the truth and which one always lies. How can the traveler find out the way to Miami by asking just one question to one of the two brothers?

333. Dynamite is a tool that can be used to cut down trees. To cut a tree 18 inches in diameter requires five sticks of dynamite—one on the north, south, east, and west sides of the tree, with the fifth stick on the side to which the tree should fall. During construction of a dam, a tree 18 inches in diameter was completely covered by water. Since the treetop was fouling the boat's propellers, it had to be cut down. A diver went down and put a stick of dynamite on the four sides of the tree. Since the current is flowing south at 2 knots per hour, on which side of the tree would you instruct the diver to put the fifth stick of dynamite if you wanted the tree to fall north?

Mystery Riddle Answers

332. The question that the traveler should ask is: Does the left road lead to Miami according to your brother? If the answer is yes, the traveler should turn right, and if the answer is no the traveler should turn left.

333. It doesn't matter where the fifth stick is placed, since the tree won't fall in any direction. Being wood, it will float and rise to the surface.

Mystery Riddles

334. Two sentries were on duty outside a barracks. One faced up the road to watch for anyone approaching from the north. The other looked down the road to see if anyone approached from the south. Suddenly one of them said to the other, "Why are you smiling?" How did he know that his companion was smiling?

335. The king dies, and two men, the true heir and an impostor, both claim to be his long-lost son. Both fit the description of the rightful heir: about the right age, height, coloring, and general appearance. Finally, one of the elders proposes a test to identify the true heir. One man agrees to the test while the other flatly refuses. The one who agreed is immediately sent on his way, and the one who refused is correctly identified as the rightful heir. Can you figure out why?

336. Four men sat down to play; they played all night till break of day. They played for gold and not for fun, with separate scores for everyone. When they had come to square accounts, they all had made quite fair amounts. Can you explain, if no one lost, how all could gain?

Mystery Riddle Answers

334. Although the guards were looking in opposite directions, they were not back to back. They were facing each other.

335. The test was a blood test. The elder remembered that the true prince was a hemophiliac.

336. The men were musicians.

Mystery Riddles

337. A woman shoots her husband, then holds him under water for 5 minutes. A little while later, they both go out and enjoy a wonderful dinner together. How can this be?

338. A man was found dead with a cassette recorder in one hand and a gun in the other. When the police came in, they immediately pressed the play button on the cassette. He said, "I have nothing else to live for. I can't go on." Then you hear the sound of a gunshot. After listening to the cassette tape, the police knew that it was not a suicide, but a homicide. How did they know?

339. An American, who had never been to any country other than the United States, travelled a long way to see a sight that very few people have seen. At one point during his trip, he stood on solid ground and saw the Great Wall of China with his own eyes. How did he do that?

340. Paul is 20 years old in 1980, but only 15 years old in 1985. How is this possible?

Mystery Riddle Answers

337. She shot her husband with a camera and then developed the photo.

338. If the man shot himself while he was recording, how did he rewind the cassette tape?

339. He was an astronaut, and he could see the Great Wall of China from where he was standing on the moon.

340. The years are in B.C., not A.D., as you probably assumed. Based on the system we use to number the years, the years counted down in B.C. (but they weren't counting backward then).

Mystery Riddles

341. A crime has been committed at Freemont Street. A man had been walking along the pathway when he was suddenly shot in the stomach. The main suspect is a man named Sean Baker. Witnesses say the suspect had brown hair and blue eyes and wore a baggy Armani suit like Sean Baker's. Sean was asked to tell the story from the beginning. "Well," said Sean, "I was just hanging around the park when I saw this man walking along the pathway. Suddenly, a guy came from behind him and shot him! I ran home as fast as I could." The policemen asked him to give a description of the murderer. Sean stated, "He had a red mustache, red hair, and a baggy Armani suit on." One of the policemen said, "I think this man is telling a lie." How did he know?

342. A couple went on a climbing trip. But only the husband returned from the vacation and said that his wife slipped while climbing and died. Upon investigating, the local sheriff arrested him saying, "Your travel agent called. You murdered your wife." The man did not inform anyone about the trip. So why was the agent so sure it is a murder?

Mystery Riddle Answers

341. How can the murderer shoot him in the stomach if he came up behind the man?

342. The man only bought a one-way ticket for his wife whereas he bought round-trip ticket for himself.

Mystery Riddles

343. A wealthy man lives alone in a small cottage. Being partially handicapped, he had everything delivered to his cottage. The mailman was delivering a letter one Thursday when he noticed that the front door was ajar. Through the opening he could see the man's body lying in a pool of dried blood. When a police officer arrived, he surveyed the scene. On the porch were two bottles of warm milk, Monday's newspaper, a catalog, flyers, and unopened mail. The police officer suspects it was foul play. Who does he suspect and why?

344. Slayer of regrets, old and new, sought by many, found by few. What am I?

345. What goes up the chimney when down, but cannot go down the chimney when up?

346. How many of each type of animal did Moses take on the Ark?

Mystery Riddle Answers

343. The police officer suspects the newspaper delivery person. The absence of Tuesday's and Wednesday's newspaper indicates that the delivery person knew there was no one there to read it.

344. Redemption.

345. An umbrella.

346. None; it was Noah that has the Ark.

Mystery Riddles

347. A dead body is found at the bottom of a multistory building. Seeing the position of the body, it is evident that the person jumped from one of the floors, committing suicide.

     A homicide detective is called to investigate the case. He goes to the first floor and walks into the room facing the direction in which the body was found.

     He opens the window in that direction and flips a coin toward the floor. Then he goes to the second floor and repeats the process. He keeps doing this until he reaches the last floor. Then, when he climbs down, he tells the team it is a murder, not suicide. How did he know that it was a murder?

348. Where can you find rivers with no water, cities with no buildings, and forests with no trees?

Mystery Riddle Answers

347. None of the windows were left open. If the person jumped, who closed the window?

348. On maps.

Mystery Riddles

349. A man owned a casino and invited some friends. It was a dark, stormy night, and they all placed their money on the table right before the lights went out. When the lights came back on, the money was gone. To find the thief, the owner put a rooster in an old, rusty tea kettle and told everyone to get in line and touch the kettle after he turned the lights off. He said the rooster would crow when the robber touched it. But after everyone touched it, the rooster didn't crow, so the man told everyone to hold out their hands. After examining all the hands, he pointed out who the robber was. How did he know who stole the money?

350. Alice is walking through the forest of forgetfulness. She wants to know what day of the week it is. She stops and asks a lion and a unicorn. Now the lion lies all of the time on Monday, Tuesday, and Wednesday. The unicorn always lies on Thursday, Friday, and Saturday. When Alice asks the lion what day it is, he says, "Well, yesterday was one of my lying days." Alice can't figure it out just from the lion's answer, so she asks the unicorn and the unicorn says, "Yesterday was also one of my lying days." What day is it?

Mystery Riddle Answers

349. Because the tea kettle was rusty, whoever touched it would have rust on their hands. The robber didn't touch the kettle; therefore, he was the only one whose hands weren't rusty.

350. Thursday.

Mystery Riddles

351. Alexander is stranded on an island covered in a forest. One day, when the wind is blowing from the west, lightning strikes the west end of the island and sets fire to the forest. The fire is very violent, burning everything in its path, and without intervention, the fire will burn the whole island, killing the man in the process. There are cliffs around the island, so he cannot jump off. How can the Alexander survive the fire when there are no buckets or any other means to put out the fire?

352. Two girls ate dinner together. They both ordered iced tea. One girl drank them very fast and finished five in the time it took the other to drink just one. All the drinks were poisoned, yet the girl who drank just one died while the other survived. How can that happen?

353. I am a five-letter word. Take away the first letter, and I am a place's name. Take away the first two letters, and I become the opposite of the five-letter word. Who am I?

Mystery Riddle Answers

351. Alexander picks up a piece of wood and lights it from the fire on the west end of the island. He then quickly carries it near the east end of the island and starts a new fire. The wind will cause that fire to burn out the eastern end and he can then shelter in the burnt area. Alexander survives the fire, but with all the food in the forest burnt, he dies of starvation.

352. The poison was in the ice, which did not melt quickly, since the tea was drank so fast.

353. Woman, oman, man.

Mystery Riddles

354. The Smith family is a very wealthy family that lives in a big, circular home. One morning, Mr. Smith woke up and found his gardener's body. He knew it was one of his employees who had killed him. So he asked them what they were doing in the morning, and he got these replies. Driver: "I was outside washing the car." Maid: "I was dusting the corners of the house." Cook: "I was starting to make lunch for later." From the replies he knew who the killer was. Can you guess who it was?

355. On the first day of school a young girl was found murdered. Police suspect four teachers and question them. They were asked what they were doing earlier that day. Mr. Walter: "I was driving to school, and I was late." Mr. Thomas: "I was checking English exam papers." Mr. Benjamin: "I was reading the newspaper." Mr. Calvin: "I was with my wife in my office." The police arrested the killer. How did the police find the murderer?

356. I have billions of eyes, yet I live in darkness. I have millions of ears, yet only four lobes. I have no muscle, yet I rule two hemispheres. What I am?

Mystery Riddle Answers

354. The maid, because they lived in a circular house, and she was apparently "dusting the corners" of the house at the time of the murder.

355. The police knew it was Mr. Thomas since he couldn't have been checking exam papers on the first day of school.

356. I am the human brain! The human brain has billions of optic and auditory nerves, four lobes and two hemispheres.

Mystery Riddles

357. A king has no sons, no daughters, and no queen, so he must decide who will take the throne after he dies. To do this, he decides that he will give all the children of the kingdom a single seed. Whichever child has the largest, most beautiful plant will earn the throne (a metaphor for building a successful kingdom). At the end of the contest all the children arrived at the palace with their enormous and beautiful plants in hand. After the king looks at all the children's pots, he finally decides that the little girl with an empty pot will be the next queen. Why did he choose this little girl over all the other children with their beautiful plants?

358. I soar without wings, I see without eyes. I've traveled the universe to and fro. I've conquered the world, yet I've never been anywhere but home. Who am I?

359. A man entered his house and was about to hang up his coat when he heard his wife shout, "No John! Don't do it!" There was a shot, and he could hear his wife fall down. When he entered the kitchen, he saw his wife and the gun lying on the floor. There was a police officer, a doctor, and a lawyer standing next to her. Peter immediately knew the police officer had shot her. But how did he know?

Mystery Riddle Answers

357. The king gave them all fake seeds. The little girl was the only honest child who didn't switch seeds.

358. I'm your imagination.

359. The police officer was the only man, while the doctor and lawyer were women. On a second glance, the husband also looked at the police officer's name tag, which read: "John." The husband's wife was saying, "No John! Don't do it!" to the police officer, and the police officer shot her anyway.

Mystery Riddles

360. A man was found dead next to a 13-story building. The police say it was a suicide, but you say it was a homicide (someone killed him). To prove this, you go to each floor on the building, open the window, and toss a penny out. You do this to each floor until you reach the 13th floor, open the window, and toss a penny out. How does this prove it wasn't a suicide?

361. A man and a woman were driving in their car when it broke down. The man decided to go for help at a gas station a few miles back. He made sure nobody was in the car, rolled all the windows up, and locked all the sedan's doors. He went off, but when he came back, his wife was dead, and there was a stranger in the car. No physical damage was done to the car, so how did the stranger get in?

362. Two men are in a desert. They both have packs on. One of the guys is dead. The guy who is alive has his pack open; the guy who is dead has his pack closed. What is in the pack?

363. There are two bodies on the floor. They are surrounded by water and broken glass. How did they die?

Mystery Riddle Answers

360. If the man committed suicide, he would have left the window open and you wouldn't have had to open it.

361. The stranger was a baby, and the woman died in childbirth.

362. A parachute (that didn't open).

363. The fish bowl got knocked over. The bodies were goldfish.

Mystery Riddles

364. A man goes out drinking every night, returning to his home in the wee hours of the morning. No matter how much he drinks, he never gets a hangover. This drink is very well known but is rarely consumed, served warm, and taken straight from its source. The man is a sucker for a free drink, especially since he can't live without it. What is his favorite drink?

365. A pet shop owner had a parrot with a sign on its cage that said "Parrot repeats everything it hears." A young man bought the parrot, and for two weeks he spoke to it and it didn't say a word. He returned the parrot, but the shopkeeper said he never lied about the parrot. How can this be?

366. Picture three boxes containing fruit. Box 1 is marked peaches, Box 2 is marked oranges, and Box 3 is marked peaches and oranges. Each of the boxes is labeled incorrectly. How could you label each box correctly if you could only select one fruit from one of the boxes?

Mystery Riddle Answers

364. Blood; he's a vampire!

365. The parrot was deaf!

366. It's possible to tell what Box 1 and Box 2 have inside them without removing a piece of fruit. Here's why: Since each is box is labeled incorrectly, then you know that Box 1, which says it contains peaches, is incorrect. This means it must have oranges in the box, not peaches. The same logic applies to Box 2. Box 3 is the only box you can't tell what's inside without removing a piece of fruit, so you need to pick one from it. Since we know the label on Box 3 is incorrect, there can only be peaches *or* oranges, not both. So, if you picked an orange, then you would know that box contains only oranges and vice versa. So, to label each box, you would label Box 3 with the type of fruit you picked from it. Then you switch the labels from Boxes 1 and 2 with each other.

Mystery Riddles

367. Two fathers and two sons went fishing one day. They were there the whole day and only caught three fish. One father said, "That is enough for all of us; we will each have one." How can this be possible?

368. Dave and Brad, two popular politicians, met at a club to discuss the overthrow of their party leader. They each ordered vodka on the rocks. Brad downed his and ordered another. He then drank his second in one gulp and decided to wait before he ordered a third. Meanwhile, Dave, who was sipping his drink, suddenly fell forward dead. Both men were set up for an assassination. Why did Dave die and Brad live?

369. A horse travels a certain distance each day. Strangely enough, two of its legs travel 30 miles each day and the other two legs travel nearly 31 miles. It would seem that two of the horse's legs must be one mile ahead of the other two legs, but, of course, this can't be true. Since the horse is normal, how is this situation possible?

Mystery Riddle Answers

367. There was the father, his son, and his son's son. This equals two fathers and two sons for a total of three!

368. Both Dave and Brad were given drinks with poisoned ice cubes. Brad drank his drinks so quickly that the ice didn't have time to melt and release the poison.

369. The horse operates a mill and travels in a circular clockwise direction. The two outside legs will travel a greater distance than the two inside legs.

Mystery Riddles

370. You are on an island in the middle of a lake. The lake is in a remote part of the country, and there has never been a bridge connecting the island to the mainland. Every day a tractor and wagon gives hay rides around the island. Puzzled as to how the tractor had gotten onto the island, you ask around and find out that the tractor was not transported to the island by boat or by air. Nor was it built on the island. Explain how the tractor got there?

371. A man went on a trip with a fox, a goose, and a sack of corn. He came upon a stream that he had to cross and found a tiny boat to use to cross the stream. He could only take himself and one other—the fox, the goose, or the corn— one at a time. He could not leave the fox alone with the goose or the goose alone with the corn. How does he get all safely over the stream?

372. A man is found hanging in a room 30 feet off the ground. There is nothing else in the room except for a large puddle of water on the ground. The police can't see any way the man could have climbed the walls to get to where he is hanging. How did this man hang himself?

Mystery Riddle Answers

370. It was driven over in winter, when the lake was frozen.

371. Take the goose over first and come back. Then take the fox over and bring the goose back. Now take the corn over and come back alone to get the goose. Take the goose over, and the job is done!

372. He stood on a tall block of ice and put the noose around his neck. Once the ice melted, he was hung, and all that was left was a puddle of water on the ground.

Mystery Riddles

373. A rich man's son was kidnapped. The ransom note told him to bring a valuable diamond to a phone booth in the middle of a public park. Plainclothes police officers surrounded the park, intending to follow the criminal or his messenger. The rich man arrived at the phone booth and followed instructions, but the police were powerless to prevent the diamond from leaving the park and reaching the crafty villain. What did he do?

374. Three mountain climbers paid a lot of money to be the first to scale a mountain. After several days of climbing they finally reached the pinnacle, and to their dismay, found a cabin and three frozen bodies. Since the mountain climbers were the first to climb the summit, how could this be possible?

375. Two convicts are locked in a cell. There is an unbarred window high up in the cell. No matter if they stand on the bed or one on top of the other, they can't reach the window to escape. So they decide to tunnel out. However, they give up on the tunneling because it will take too long. Finally one of the convicts figures out how to escape from the cell. What is his plan?

Mystery Riddle Answers

373. This is a true story from Taiwan. When the rich man reached the phone booth, he found a carrier pigeon in a cage. It had a message attached telling the man to put the diamond in a small bag, which was around the pigeon's neck, and to release the bird. When the man did this, the police were powerless to follow the bird as it returned across the city to its owner.

374. They found a cabin of an airplane that had crashed with three bodies in it.

375. His plan is to dig the tunnel, pile the dirt up to the window, then climb up it to escape.

Mystery Riddles

376. It was a man's birthday. He lay dead in the living room of his house. Next to his body was a note written in pencil. The note read "Happy Birthday, Friend." The victim had a girlfriend, and the police suspected her ex-boyfriend but they could find no obvious evidence. While searching the ex-boyfriend's car, the police saw an envelope with the girlfriend's address written on it. They had the handwriting checked against the note. The scientist in charge came in early to work the next day; it was 7 a.m. He looked out his window, which faced east, and stared at the rising sun. It was then that he realized how to prove the ex-boyfriend killed the man, even though the girlfriend's address was not written in the same handwriting. How did he do it?

377. A couple went on holiday for three weeks. They carefully locked their house and had a neighbor check on the place while they were gone. When they returned, the wife was distressed to learn that because of a power failure she had lost all her fine jewelry. She had hidden the jewelry in what she thought was a safe place. She was not robbed; her jewelry was lost by accident. Why?

Mystery Riddle Answers

376. The scientist's office faced east, and the sun was coming in through the window at a very low angle. He saw some faint shadows on the surface of the envelope. He looked closer. There were the words embossed on the paper. They read "Happy Birthday, Friend." The ex-boyfriend had forgotten that a pencil leaves an impression on paper beneath the page it is written on.

377. In this true incident, the wife had hidden her best jewelry inside her freezer in a bag among all the frozen food. Because of a general power failure, the freezer had shut off. A friendly neighbor (who had a key in order to water the plants) had tried to be helpful by throwing out all the bad food— and with it went the jewelry.

Mystery Riddles

378. You have two sand hourglasses, one that measures 4 minutes and one that measures 7 minutes. You need to measure 2 minutes to boil an egg. Using only these two hourglasses, how can you measure 2 minutes to boil your egg?

379. A guy is waiting at home, when he swings a metal pole, then takes three left turns. On his way back home, there is a masked man waiting for him. What is he doing, and who is the masked man?

Mystery Riddle Answers

378. Flip over both hourglasses at the same time.

    After 4 minutes, the 4-minute hourglass will be done, and there will be 3 minutes left in the 7-minute hourglass. Immediately flip the 4-minute hourglass over again.

    After 3 more minutes, the 7-minute hourglass will be done, and there will be 1 minute left in the 4-minute hourglass. Immediately flip the 7-minute hourglass over again.

    After 1 more minute, the 4-minute hourglass will be done again, and there will be 6 minutes left in the 7-minute hourglass. Immediately flip over the 4-minute hourglass.

    After 4 more minutes, the 4-minute hourglass will be done again, and there will be 2 minutes left in the 7-minute hourglass. At this point, put your egg in the boiling water. When the 7-minute hourglass is done, it will have been 2 more minutes, and your egg will have boiled just right.

379. He is playing baseball, and the masked man is the catcher.

Difficult Riddles

380. When you look in my face, I will look you in the eye, and I will never lie. What am I?

381. My thunder comes before my lightning. My lightning comes before my rain. And my rain dries all the ground it touches. What am I?

382. A man was cleaning the windows of a 20-story building. He slipped and fell off the ladder, but wasn't hurt. How did he do it?

383. What king can you make if you take the head of a lamb, the middle of a pig, the hind of a buffalo, and the tail of a dragon?

384. What was significant about 3,661 seconds past midnight on January 1, 2001?

385. Reaching stiffly for the sky, I bare my fingers when it's cold. In warmth I wear an emerald glove, and in between I dress in gold.

386. A girl is sitting in a house at night that has no lights. There is no lamp, no candle, no light at all. Yet she is reading. How?

Difficult Riddle Answers

380. Your reflection.

381. A volcano.

382. He fell off the second step.

383. A lion. The head of a Lamb, the middle of a pIg, the hind of a buffalO, and the tail of a dragoN.

384. The time and date was 01:01:01 on 01/01/01.

385. A deciduous tree.

386. The girl is blind, and she is reading Braille.

Difficult Riddles

387. NASA was considering sending canaries into space to study them under zero gravity. The project was scrapped when someone realized that in spite of having sufficient water supplies, they could die of dehydration within a few hours. Why?

388. Mr. and Mrs. Smith were walking home from the shopping mall with their purchases when Mr. Smith began to complain that his load was too heavy. Mrs. Smith turned to her husband and said, "I don't know what you're complaining about, because if you gave me one of your parcels, I would have twice as many as you, and if I gave you just one of mine, we would have equal loads." How many parcels was each carrying?

389. Why is the letter A the most like a flower?

390. What is in front of a man and at the back of a farm?

391. What question can someone ask all day long, always get completely different answers, and yet all the answers could be correct?

Difficult Riddle Answers

387. Birds, unlike humans, need gravity to swallow. Humans can swallow even while hanging upside down.

388. Mrs. Smith was carrying seven parcels, and Mr. Smith was carrying five.

389. Because the B is after it.

390. The letter M.

391. What time is it?

Difficult Riddles

392. There is a barrel with no lid and some wine in it. "The barrel of wine is more than half full," said Curly. "No it's not," says Mo. "It's less than half full." Without any measuring implements and without removing any wine from the barrel, how can they easily determine who is correct?

393. On a fine sunny day a ship was in the harbor. All of a sudden the ship began to sink. There was no storm, and nothing wrong with the ship, yet it sank in front of the spectators' eyes. What caused the ship to sink?

394. Which does not belong in this group: apple, grape, banana, cherry, or the pear?

395. Thirty white horses are on a red hill. First they champ, then they stamp, then they stand still. What are they?

396. Use the letters O O U S W T D N E J R to spell just one word. What is it?

397. A woman visited her bank manager, and she took her young daughter with her. The bank manager said that the woman's daughter could stay with his secretary during the meeting. When the woman and her daughter left, the secretary turned to the other secretary and said, "That little girl was my daughter." How could that be?

Difficult Riddle Answers

392. Tilt the barrel until the wine barely touches the lip. If the bottom of the barrel is visible then it is less than half full. If the barrel bottom is still completely covered by the wine, then it is more than half full.

393. It was a submarine.

394. The banana. It's the only one that needs to be peeled before eating.

395. Teeth.

396. Just one word.

397. The secretary was the girl's father.

Difficult Riddles

398.   If you're 8 feet away from a door, and with each move, you advance half the distance to the door, how many moves will it take to reach the door?

399.   The marathon man timed himself and found out that if he wore a bright white outfit, he ran 20 miles in 80 minutes, but when he wore a dark outfit, he ran 20 miles in one hour and 20 minutes. What does this mean for his next race?

400.   A psychologist goes to a village in Africa and decides to compare foot size to intelligence. He notes that in general, as foot size increases, so does intelligence. How can this be?

401.   A murderer is condemned to death. He has to choose between three rooms. The first is full of raging fires, the second is full of assassins with loaded guns, and the third is full of lions that haven't eaten in three years. Which room is safest?

402.   How do you spell candy in two letters?

Difficult Riddle Answers

398. You will never reach the door. It will always be half the distance, no matter how small!

399. Absolutely nothing, as 80 minutes equals an hour and 20 minutes.

400. He is measuring everyone's feet, including the feet of the very small children. So the statistics will show that larger feet belong to the smarter people, the adults.

401. The third. Lions that haven't eaten in three years are dead.

402. C and y; c(and)y.

Difficult Riddles

403. What was the biggest island in the world before the discovery of Australia by Captain Cook?

404. When you went into the woods, you got me. You hated me yet you wanted to find me. You went home with me because you couldn't find me. What was it?

405. There is a frog, dead in the middle of an island. If he swims north, the distance to the mainland is 2 miles. If he swims south, the distance to the mainland is 3 miles. If he swims east or west, the distance is 4 miles. Which way does he swim?

406. George, Helen, and Steve are drinking coffee. Bert, Karen, and Dave are drinking soda. Is Elizabeth drinking coffee or soda?

407. A black dog stands in the middle of an intersection in a town painted black. None of the street lights are working due to a power failure caused by a storm. A car with two broken headlights drives toward the dog but turns in time to avoid hitting him. How could the driver have seen the dog in time?

408. We hurt without moving and poison without touching. We bear truth and lies, but we are not judged by size. What are we?

Difficult Riddle Answers

403. Australia was always the biggest island in the world, even before it was discovered.

404. A splinter.

405. He doesn't swim at all; he is dead.

406. Elizabeth is drinking coffee. The letter E appears twice in her name, as it does in the names of the others who are drinking coffee.

407. Who said this happened during the night?

408. Words.

Difficult Riddles

409.   What is as light as a feather, but even the world's strongest man couldn't hold it for more than 5 minutes?

410.   In a one-story blue house, there was a blue person, a blue cat, a blue fish, a blue chair, a blue table, a blue sink, a blue shower—everything was blue. What color were the stairs?

411.   I'm teary-eyed but never cry. Silver-tongued, but never lie. Double-winged, but never fly. Air-cooled, but never dry. What am I?

412.   A sundial is the type of timepiece that has the fewest moving parts. What type of timepiece has the most moving parts?

413.   I am found in the sea and on land but I do not walk or swim. I travel by foot but I am toeless. No matter where I go, I'm never far from home. What am I?

414.   I always follow my brother, although very different we are. You can see him, but not me. You can hear me, but not him. What am I?

Difficult Riddle Answers

409. His breath.

410. There were not any stairs; it was a one-story house!

411. Mercury. The element is wet, and it looks shiny and silver. The god Mercury has two wings but only uses them to run.

412. An hourglass.

413. A snail.

414. Thunder and lightning.

Difficult Riddles

415. What has six faces but does not wear makeup. It also has 21 eyes but cannot see?

416. Samuel was out for a walk when it started to rain. He did not have an umbrella, and he wasn't wearing a hat. His clothes were soaked, yet not a single hair on his head got wet. How could this happen?

417. Why are manholes round instead of square?

418. Tom and his younger sister were fighting. Their mother was tired of the fighting and decided to punish them by making them stand on the same piece of newspaper, but she fashioned it so they were unable to touch each other. How did she accomplish this?

419. I cut through evil like a double-edged sword, and chaos flees at my approach. Through battles fought with heart and mind, balance I single-handedly upraise, instead of with my gaze. What am I?

420. I weaken all men for hours each day. I show you strange visions while you are away. I take you by night. By day, I take you back. None suffer to have me, but do from my lack. What am I?

Difficult Riddle Answers

415. A die (dice).

416. This man is bald!

417. If they're square it's possible for the cover to slip down the hole (diagonally). A round manhole cannot fall down no matter which way it is rotated because it's width in any direction is greater than the opening on the hole.

418. Tom's mother slid a newspaper under a door and told each sibling to stand on either side.

419. Justice.

420. Sleep.

Difficult Riddles

421. Placed above it, it makes greater things small. Placed beside it, it makes small things greater. In matters that count it always comes first. Where others increase it, it keeps all things the same. What is it?

422. Brad stared through the dirty, soot-smeared window on the 22nd floor of the office tower. Overcome with depression, he slid the window open and jumped through it. It was a sheer drop outside the building to the ground. Miraculously after he landed, he was completely unhurt. Since there was nothing to cushion his fall or slow his descent, how could he have survived the fall?

423. If you screw a light bulb into a socket by turning the bulb toward the right with your right hand, which way would you turn the socket with your left hand to unscrew it while holding the bulb stationary?

424. What is it that has a bottom at the top of them?

Difficult Riddle Answers

421. The number 1.

422. Brad was so sick and tired of window washing, he opened the window and jumped inside.

423. To the right. It's always the same direction.

424. Your legs.

Difficult Riddles

425. A man wanted to enter an exclusive club but did not know the password that was required. He waited by the door, and listened. A club member knocked on the door and the doorman said, "twelve." The member replied, "six " and was let in. A second member came to the door and the doorman said, "six." The member replied, "three" and was let in. The man thought he had heard enough and walked up to the door. The doorman said, "ten" and the man replied, "five." But he was not let in. What should have he said?

426. A man takes a barrel that weighs 20 pounds, then puts something in it. It now weighs less than 20 pounds. What did he put in the barrel?

427. What is the easiest way to throw a ball, have it stop, and completely reverse direction after traveling a short distance?

428. A beggar's brother died, but the man who died had no brother. How could this be?

429. I'm pleasing to the eye and a tool for many absent of mind. A tapestry of fickle lies blind to even the most pensive spies. I'm often the breeder of fervent lust, but I am by far one you shouldn't trust?

Difficult Riddle Answers

425. Three. The doorman lets in those who answer with the number of letters in the word the doorman says.

426. He put a hole in the barrel to make it weigh less.

427. Toss it in the air.

428. The beggar was a woman.

429. Appearance.

Difficult Riddles

430. The first man is the master of priceless gems. The second man is the master of love. The third man is the master of shovels. The fourth man is the master of big sticks. Who are they?

431. A dad and his son were riding in a car and crashed. Two ambulances came and took them to different hospitals. The man's son was in the operating room, and the doctor said, "I can't operate on you. You're my son." How is that possible?

432. A train pulls in alongside a crowded platform. It is precisely on schedule. The train is not full, and yet nobody boards it. All trains that stop at the platform travel to the same destinations. Why then did nobody board the train?

433. Gaze at this sentence for just about 60 seconds, then explain what makes it quite different from the average sentence.

Difficult Riddle Answers

430. The kings in a deck of cards.

431. The doctor is his mother.

432. It is a model train.

433. It contains all of the letters in the alphabet.

Difficult Riddles

434. Monday, Sam and Ralph went to a restaurant to eat lunch. After eating lunch, they paid the bill. But Sam and Ralph did not pay the bill, so who did?

435. A house has four walls. All the walls are facing south, and a bear is circling the house. What color is the bear?

436. What eight-letter word can have a letter taken away and it still makes a word. Take another letter away and it still makes a word. Keep on doing that until you have one letter left. What is the word?

437. A boy was at a carnival and went to a booth where a man said to the boy, "If I write your exact weight on this piece of paper, then you have to give me $50, but if I cannot, I will pay you $50." The boy looked around and saw no scale, so he agrees, thinking no matter what the carny writes, he'll just say he weighs more or less. In the end the boy ended up paying the man $50. How did the man win the bet?

438. It can't be seen, can't be felt, can't be heard, and can't be smelled. It lies behind stars and under hills, and empty holes it fills. It comes first and follows after, ends after life, and kills laughter. What is it?

Difficult Riddle Answers

434. Their friend, Monday.

435. The house is on the North Pole, so the bear is white.

436. The word is starting! Starting, staring, string, sting, sing, sin, in, I. Cool, huh?

437. The man did exactly as he said he would and wrote "your exact weight" on the paper.

438. A shadow.

Difficult Riddles

439. What starts off moving on four legs, then two, and finally three?

440. What belongs to you, but others use it more than you do?

441. Can you name three consecutive days without using the words Monday, Tuesday, Wednesday, Thursday, Friday, Saturday, or Sunday?

442. What's 3/7 chicken, 2/3 cat, and 2/4 goat?

443. Suppose you want to send a valuable object to a friend in the mail. You have a box that is big enough to hold the object. The box has a locking ring that is large enough to have a lock attached, and you have several locks with keys. However, your friend does not have the key to any lock that you have. You cannot send the key in an unlocked box, since it may be stolen or copied. How do you send the valuable object, locked, to your friend, so it may be opened by your friend?

444. What seven-letter word becomes longer when the third letter is removed?

Difficult Riddle Answers

439. A human being. (A baby crawls on four legs and later walks on two legs. When they are old, they use a cane, which acts as the third leg.)

440. Your name.

441. Yesterday, today, and tomorrow.

442. Chicago. In chicken, the first three letters out of seven are CHI. In cat, the first two letters out of three are CA. And in goat, the first two letters out of four are GO. Put it all together, and you have: (CHI)(CA)(GO).

443. Send the box with a lock attached and locked. Your friend attaches their lock and sends the box back to you. You remove your lock and send it back to your friend. Your friend may then remove the lock they put on and open the box.

444. Lounger.

Difficult Riddles

445.   A pregnant lady named her children: Dominique, Regis, Michelle, Fawn, Sophie, and Lara. What will she name her next child? Jessica, Katie, Abby, or Tilly?

446.   Five apples are in a basket. How do you divide them among five girls so that each girl gets an apple, but one apple remains in the basket?

447.   We are little creatures; all of us have different features. One of us in glass is set; one of us you'll find in jet. Another you may see in tin, and the fourth is boxed within. If the fifth you should pursue, it can never fly from you. What are we?

448.   There are eight people on a small boat at sea, and nobody is below deck, yet there's not a single person in sight. How is this possible?

449.   What type of cheese is made backward?

450.   What seven-letter word is spelled the same way backward and forward?

451.   A sphere has three, a circle has two, and a point has zero. What is it?

Difficult Riddle Answers

445. Tilly. She seems to follow the scale do, re, me, fa, so, la, and then ti.

446. Give the fifth girl her apple in the basket.

447. We are vowels.

448. They are all married.

449. Edam.

450. Racecar.

451. Dimensions.

Difficult Riddles

452. Three playing cards are in a row. Can you name them with these clues? There is a two to the right of a king. A diamond will be found to the left of a spade. An ace is to the left of a heart. A heart is to the left of a spade. Now, identify all three cards.

453. Two mothers and two daughters go shopping. They have $21, which they split equally between them. How can this be possible?

454. Ten pears hanging high, 10 men come passing by. Each took a pear and left nine hanging there. How could that be?

455. A sharpshooter hung up his hat and put on a blindfold. He then walked 100 yards, turned around, and shot a bullet through his hat. The blindfold was a perfectly good one, completely blocking the man's vision. How did he manage this?

456. A truck driver is going the opposite way of traffic on a one-way street. A police officer sees him but doesn't stop him. Why didn't the police officer stop him?

Difficult Riddle Answers

452. Ace of diamonds, king of hearts, two of spades.

453. There are only three people. One of the mothers is a daughter also, because there is a grandmother, a mother and a daughter! They each get $7.

454. Each is the name of one of the men, and he's the only one who took a pear.

455. He hung is hat on the barrel of his gun.

456. He is walking.

Difficult Riddles

457. The 22nd and 24th presidents of the United States had the same parents but were not brothers. How can this be possible?

458. Four cars come to a four-way stop, all coming from a different direction. They can't decide who got there first, so they all go forward at the same time. They do not crash into each other, but all four cars go. How is this possible?

459. Dead on the field lie 10 soldiers in white, felled by three eyes, black as night. What happened?

460. I can sizzle like bacon; I am made with an egg. I have plenty of backbone, but lack a good leg. I peel layers like onions, but still remain whole. I can be long, like a flagpole, yet fit in a hole. What am I?

461. In a certain city, 5 percent of all the persons in town have unlisted phone numbers. If you select 100 names at random from that city's phone directory, how many people selected will have unlisted phone numbers?

Difficult Riddle Answers

457. They were the same man. Grover Cleveland served two terms as president of the United States, but the terms were not consecutive.

458. They all made right-hand turns.

459. A strike was thrown in 10-pin bowling.

460. A snake.

461. None. If their names are in the phone directory, they do not have unlisted phone numbers!

Difficult Riddles

462. A woman in a car stopped and looked outside. She saw a black door, a white door, and a red door. Which door did she open first?

463. Jason stands tall at 6 feet. He works at a box company and wears size 13 shoes. What does he weigh?

464. How do you spell cow in 13 letters?

465. A smooth dance, a ball sport, a place to stay, an Asian country, and a girl's name. What's her name?

466. If a train was on its way to Florida, and it tipped over, where would they bury the survivors?

467. There is a word in the English language in which the first two letters signify a male, the first three letters signify a female, the first four letters signify a great man, and the whole word signifies, a great woman. What is the word?

468. Two men were playing tennis. They played five sets, and each man won three sets. How can this be possible?

Difficult Riddle Answers

462. The car door.

463. Boxes

464. SEE O DOUBLE YOU.

465. Juliet. All the listed things describe a part of the NATO phonetic alphabet: foxtrot, golf, hotel, India, and finally Juliet.

466. They wouldn't need to; the survivors are still alive!

467. Heroine.

468. The two men were partners playing doubles.

Difficult Riddles

469. How is it that a person born in Massachusetts, whose parents were both born in Massachusetts, is not born a U.S. Citizen?

470. A magician was boasting one day about how long he could hold his breath under water. His record was 6 minutes. A kid that was listening said, "That's nothing, I can stay under water for 10 minutes using no equipment or air pockets!" The magician told the kid if he could do that, he'd give him $10,000. The kid did it and won the money. Can you figure out how?

471. There are four brothers in this world that were all born together. The first runs and never wearies. The second eats and is never full. The third drinks and is always thirsty. The fourth sings a song that is never good. What are the four brothers?

472. There are 20 people in an empty, square room. Each person has full sight of the entire room and everyone in it without turning their head or body, or moving in any way (other than their eyes). Where can you place an apple so that all but one person can see it?

Difficult Riddle Answers

469. If he was born before 1783, then Massachusetts would still be a British colony.

470. The kid filled a glass of water and held it over his head for 10 minutes.

471. Water, fire, earth, and wind.

472. Place the apple on one person's head.

Difficult Riddles

473. You walk up to a mountain that has two paths. One leads to the other side of the mountain, and the other will get you lost forever. Two twins know the path that leads to the other side. You can ask them only one question, except one lies and one tells the truth, and you don't know which is which. So, what do you ask?

474. Romeo and Juliet are found dead on the floor in a bedroom. When they were discovered, there were pieces of glass and some water on the floor. The only furniture in the room is a shelf and a bed. The house is in a remote location, away from everything except for the nearby railroad track. What caused the death of Romeo and Juliet?

475. You are in a room that is completely bricked in on all sides, including the ceiling and floor. You have nothing but a mirror and a wooden table in the room with you. How do you get out?

476. Our dinner guests cry that we are evil, when they notice their place in the meal. But it's no big deal; we are just one big, happy tribe! And we get really fed up with people! Who, what, or are we?

Difficult Riddle Answers

473. You ask each twin, "What would your brother say?" Here's how it works: Let's say the correct path is on the left. You ask the liar, "What would your brother say?" The liar would know his brother was honest and he would say the left, but since the liar lies, he would say the right. If you asked the honest twin the same question, he would say the right, because he knows his brother will lie. Therefore, you would know that the correct path was on the left!

474. Romeo and Juliet are fish. The rumble of the train knocked the tank off the shelf. It broke, and Romeo and Juliet did not survive.

475. You look in the mirror, and you see what you saw. You take the saw, and you cut the table in half. Two halves make a whole, and you climb out the hole.

476. Cannibals!

Difficult Riddles

477. My sister has two children. I had two children. My brother has two children. My cousin has two children. Wow, that's a lot of children! How many children are there in all?

478. What five-letter word is something you get from the sun if you remove the first letter? If you remove the second letter, you get something to eat. If you remove third letter, you get a word you use for pointing at, and if you remove the fourth letter, you get something to drink. What is it?

479. In marble walls as white as milk, lined with skin as soft as silk, within a fountain crystal clear, a golden apple does appear. No doors are in this stronghold, yet thieves break in and steal the gold.

480. A man and his son were driving to meet their mom when they got in a car wreck. On the way to the ER, the man passed away. The surgeon said I can't operate on this boy; he is my son. How can this be?

481. Some say we are red, some say we are green. Some play us, some spray us. What are we?

Difficult Riddle Answers

477.   There are six children. If you said eight children, you are wrong! I had two children refers to the past tense.

478.   Wheat. Wheat, heat, eat, tea.

479.   An egg.

480.   The surgeon is the mom.

481.   Pepper.

Difficult Riddles

482. Before any changes I'm a garlic or spice. My first is altered, and I'm a hand-warming device. My second is changed, and I'm trees in full bloom. The next letter change makes a deathly old tomb. Change the fourth to make a fruit of the vine. Change the last for a chart plotted with lines. What was I? What did I become? What did I turn out to be?

483. I was born in the 18th century, yet still live on today. I appear on TV when I have something to say. Called everything from honest to a dirty rotten crook, I used to wear a wig, but I've had several looks. I've always had a party but never disturb the neighbors. I've been shot at many times—major stories for the papers. What am I?

484. Here on Earth it's always true that a day follows a day. But there is a place where yesterday always follows today!

485. If three cats catch three mice in 3 minutes, how many cats would be needed to catch 100 mice in 100 minutes?

Difficult Riddle Answers

482. Clove, glove, grove, grave, grape, graph.

483. The office of the president of the United States.

484. In a dictionary.

485. The same three cats would do. Since these three cats are averaging one mouse per minute, given 100 minutes, the cats could catch 100 mice.

Difficult Riddles

486. A hiker comes to a fork in the road and doesn't know which way to go to reach his destination. There are two men at the fork, one of whom always tells the truth while the other always lies. The hiker doesn't know which is which, though. He may ask one of the men only one question to find his way. Which man does he ask, and what is the question?

487. It looks like water, but it is heat. Sits on sand, but lays on concrete. People have been known to follow it everywhere but it gets them no place, and all they can do is stare.

488. A woman was horrified to find a fly in her tea. The waiter took her cup and went into the kitchen and returned with a fresh cup of tea. She shouted, "You brought me the same tea!" How did she know?

489. The answer I give is yes, but what I mean is no. What was the question?

Difficult Riddle Answers

486.   Either man should be asked the following question: If I were to ask you if this is the way I should go, would you say yes? While asking the question, the hiker should be pointing at either of the directions going from the fork.

487.   A mirage.

488.   Sugar. She had already put sugar in it, and when she tasted the new tea, it was already sweet.

489.   Do you mind?

Difficult Riddles

490.   The following sentence is false. The preceding sentence is true. Are these sentences true or false?

491.   I am black of eye and bright of hair, and my feet are firmly in the ground. I love the sun upon my face, and I follow it around. When I am dead and gone, it's said that I will droop real low, standing stiff within my row, and keep the birds well fed. What am I?

492.   Which clock works best—the one that loses a minute a day or the one that doesn't work at all?

493.   It's true I bring serenity and hang around the stars, but I live in misery. You'll find me behind bars with the thieves and villains I consort. In prison I'll be found, but I would never go to court, unless, of course, there's more than one.

Difficult Riddle Answers

490. Neither; it's a paradox. If the first is true, then the second must be false, which makes the first false. So, it doesn't work.

491. A sunflower.

492. The one that doesn't work is best as it will always be correct twice a day, but the one that loses a minute a day will not be correct again for 720 days (losing 720 minutes or 12 hours).

493. The letter S.

Difficult Riddles

494. Three robbers robbed a store. Once they came out, they were totally changed, but they still continued robbing. Why?

495. A young boy needs to cross a bridge that can only hold 100 pounds of weight. The young boy weighs 98 pounds. The young boy also has three balls that each weigh 1 pound each. The young boy needs to get across the bridge with all the balls at the exact same time. How does he get across the bridge with all three balls at the same time?

496. A person was building a house, and then it fell down. He did not get hurt or mad because he knew it was going to fall, and he did not expect anyone to live in it. What happened?

497. Shortly after jumping from an aircraft at 5,000 or so feet, a man deploys his parachute. When he looks up, he sees a rather large hole in his parachute. Nonetheless he lands safely without assistance and without using his reserve chute. Why did he survive?

498. Can you guess the next letter in the series?
CYGTNLIT

Difficult Riddle Answers

494. They robbed a clothing store; they changed clothes, not their ways.

495. The boy juggles all three balls while he walks across the bridge.

496. The person was a little boy who was building a house of cards!

497. Most parachutes need a hole in them to let the air pass through. Otherwise the parachute would swing wildly from side to side.

498. S—Can You Guess The...

Difficult Riddles

499. There once was a man who lived in a house, and every time he went to bed, he turned on the light. One night, the man forgot to turn on the light. The next day he read the paper and had to run away. Why?

500. In a pond there are some flowers with some bees hovering over the flowers. How many flowers and bees are there if both the following statements are true: 1) If each bee lands on a flower, one bee doesn't get a flower. 2) If two bees share each flower, there is one flower left out.

501. A man was to be sentenced, and the judge told him you may make a statement. "If you tell the truth, I'll sentence you to four years, however, if you lie, then I'll sentence you to six years." After the man's statement, the judge decides to let him go. What did the man say?

Difficult Riddle Answers

499. The man lived in a lighthouse. He forgot to turn on the light and a ship crashed. The next morning he read in the paper that the ship crashed, and he killed himself because he felt guilty.

500. Four bees and three flowers.

501. "You will sentence me to six years." If that statement was a lie, the man would get six years which would really make his statement true. If it was true, he would only get four years rendering the statement false. Refusing to go against his own word the judge decides to let him go.

Difficult Riddles

502. Jody likes grapes but not potatoes. She likes squash but not lettuce, and she likes peas but not onions. Following the same rule, will she like pumpkins or oranges?

503. A woman is sitting in her hotel room when there is a knock at the door. She opened the door to see a man whom she had never seen before. He said, "Oh I'm sorry, I have made a mistake. I thought this was my room." He then went down the corridor and into the elevator. The woman went back into her room and phoned security. What made the woman so suspicious of the man?

504. When I am first stated, I am quite mysterious, but when I am revealed, I'm nothing serious. What am I?

Difficult Riddle Answers

502. Pumpkins. Jody only likes things that grow on vines.

503. You don't knock on your own hotel door, and the man did.

504. A riddle.

Thank you for reading *Riddles and Brain Teasers for Clever Kids*. If you would please take a few minutes to write a brief review on Amazon, it would be greatly appreciated.

Made in the USA
Columbia, SC
05 April 2020